ATTITUDE AT WORK

How To Give Yourself Permission to Love Your Job

Olayinka Joseph

Author of
Serendipity: The Miracle You Pray For May Not Be The Miracle You Get!

ATTITUDE AT WORK

How To Give Yourself Permission to Love Your Job

Olayinka Joseph

Author of
Serendipity: The Miracle You Pray For May Not Be The Miracle You Get!

This book is available at a special discount when ordered in bulk quantities.

For information, contact Olayinka Joseph and Indigo Riverbank Books, TX
P.O. Box 721791,
Houston Texas 77272-1791.
Tel: (713) 283-5141

ISBN: 0-9700236-8-5

Printed in the United States of America

TABLE OF CONTENT

OTHER BOOKS BY OLAYINKA JOSEPH

1) Serendipity: *The Miracle You Pray For May Not Be The Miracle Your Get* - 2010
2) Is There A Book In You? *How To Prepare, Write And Publish Your Book in 90 Days or Less* - 2010
3) I Dare You! *To Beat The Odds Against You* - 2008
4) Wind of Change In The Air – *Can't You Feel It*? - 2006
5) Turn Your Accent Into An Asset – *How To Deliver A Dynamic Speech Even If English Is Not Your First Language* - 2006
6) I Would Save Mama First – *A Celebration of Motherhood* - 2005
7) Soaring On The Wings of Courage – *The Art of Self Encouragement* – 2001
8) Voices of Courage – *Everyone Has a Story* - 2000

FOREWORD

Work is essential to life and to making a living. What kind of work you do or how you make a living can be a choice. Whether you love what you do or not, your attitude at work will determine whether you have good days or bad days.

Olayinka Joseph's careful analysis of how an improvement in attitude about work can change one's life is full of insight. Millions of people are unemployed or working in jobs they did not choose. Joseph cautions against allowing the environment to control you and provides tactical ways and useful tips for you to learn how to control your environment.

By taking these carefully recommended steps, you can improve your attitude, enjoy your work, and get positive results. The final outcome of an improved attitude is better health, more productivity and more income—the goal of all work. This book is a YES!

Naomi Mitchell Carrier,
Author of Go Down, Old Hannah
www.godownoldhannah.com

ATTITUDE AT WORK

Introduction

To put the world right in order, we must first put the nation in order; to put the nation in order, we must first put the family in order; to put the family in order, we must first cultivate our personal and professional life. To cultivate our personal and professional life, we must first set our hearts right. To set our hearts right, we must first watch our attitude. Now that's ATTITUDE TALK!

A study by William James of Harvard University found that when a person gets a job, 85% of the time, it is because of his or her attitude, and only 15% of the time because of how smart he or she is and how many facts and figures that person knows.

A positive attitude is crucial to establishing and maintaining personal effectiveness, responsibility, credibility and accountability in the workplace.

Your attitude affects every part of your being – relationships, your success in life, your outlook on life and how you respond or react to what happens to you on a daily basis.

Your attitude makes all the difference!

In *Attitude At Work*, you will learn some tips that will help you develop positive attitudes even when you don't feel like it. You will also get tips on how to encourage a positive attitude and/or how to deal with a negative attitude.

As my grandmother used to say, "Having a negative attitude is like going to the river in a leaking boat to fish." Very soon the boat will take on water and you'll find yourself in the water. Good attitudes, however, lead to good relationships with co-workers and makes for a happy workplace.

-Olayinka Joseph

Chapter 1

PERMIT YOURSELF TO LOVE YOUR JOB

I ought to consider my job a blessing – not a curse.

- Theodore Huggenvik

My great-grandfather was a hunter, farmer and fisherman. My grandfather was a hunter and fisherman. My father was a fisherman. I, for one, left home at the age of nine because I didn't want to be a fisherman like my father, or a hunter and farmer like my grandfather and/or a hunter, farmer and fisherman like my great-grandfather.

Not because there was anything wrong about being a fisherman, hunter or farmer – in fact, those were and are still viable professions. I left because I had a choice.

In those days, people were more concerned about survival. Today, however, we have many more opportunities to choose from than our fathers, grandfathers and great-grandfathers.

Work ran in the family. You did the same work your father before you or you learned a different trade that the community had a need of.

Today, however, you don't have to be a "bricklayer" just because your father and your grandfather mixed cement, sand and gravel. You don't have to become a mine worker just because that's the only work that your community seems to have a current need for. I didn't have to become a fisherman just because that was what all the people in my village knew how to do.

In fact, there are millions of possible trades and professions for you to choose from. There are no restrictions, especially if you have proper training in the trade or profession you desire.

It is not impossible to find the son of a miner who is now a medical doctor or the daughter of a factory worker who is now an Associate Justice of the Supreme Court of the United States, even though their parents had little or no education.

All these opportunities were made possible because these people had a choice unlike their fathers and mothers.

The most interesting thing, however, is that although we have this array of professions and trades to choose from; we have freedom to choose what we want to do, and we have no restrictions whatsoever as to what we choose to do. Most importantly, we make these choices without compulsion; many people still end up resenting, hating, and complaining about their jobs with a passion at some point in the course of their professional life.

One cannot help but ask the obvious question. "Why?"

Why would someone choose a profession, but fail to have the drive and the enthusiasm to give it everything he's got? Why would employees go to the extent of sabotaging their employers who pay their salaries and wages? Why is it that labor is always at loggerhead with management? In short, why do people have negative attitudes at work?

Studies have shown two prominent reasons why some people resent their jobs:

In *Secrets of Executive Success* by Rodale Center for Executive Development, one of the reasons is the fact that many people feel they are being forced to work to earn a living instead of spending time doing what they really love to do (like enjoying themselves on the beach or at an exotic location somewhere halfway around the world).

This feeling of powerlessness usually culminates into some level of negative attitude toward work, which leads to resentment resulting in an employee doing just want needs to be done to keep the job.

One interesting thing about this state-of-mind is that if you gave people like that a chance to take a vacation for an extended period of time (for instance, three months), by halfway through that period, they would go out of their minds. They would be wishing they were back at work. They would be anxious to become productive, creative and active again.

The point is that while all work and no play is not good, all play and no work is equally disastrous. We need to feel that we are accomplishing something tangible or something of value to maintain self dignity and a sense of worth.

The second reason for the resentment many people have for their jobs is the fact that they feel trapped. It is true that at the beginning of employment (like straight out of college) people have a choice of different professions. I did. I worked for three oil companies and a bank within the first six years of my leaving college.

However, after spending a few years doing a job, people begin to gather attachments like a wife, children, a home, professional associations, social clubs and other responsibilities, which make pulling away from the job very difficult.

According to basic economics, spending time doing a job over and over again leads to specialization and experience. The resultant effect is that after gaining such experience and becoming specialized, it becomes very difficult for people to veer off into other professions. This leads to the feeling of being trapped because the job has become monotonous. It has lost its passion.

If this individual cannot find a way to be inspired or motivated, the feeling of powerlessness and poor attitude sets in, and may lead to self sabotage.

I recently met a young man of about 22 years of age – a very brilliant young man! During our conversation, I discovered that he wanted to help immigrants from South America launch small businesses in America.

When I asked him why he wasn't doing that, his shoulders visibly dropped. His voice quivered as he said, "Because I was stupid at one point."

He said he was doing very well financially when he was in high school. He had a small business selling items at the flea market. He would buy things wholesale and sell them retail. According to him, there were weekends when he made over $500 in profit.

Instead of keeping the money, he would load his friends in his car, and they would go to nightclubs where they picked up girls and bought them expensive gifts.

Straight out of high school, he got married and had a child. He moved out of his parent's home and got his own apartment.

He went on to tell me that he would like to have a business like the one he was working in and be a consultant, but he wasn't sure when that day would come because of the responsibilities he now had. In other words, this young man felt trapped in his job. He felt like he should be flying instead of driving.

Thank goodness, even though he was feeling trapped, he was still enjoying his job. It was still paying his bills. But I was afraid his feelings would go south as his responsibilities increased and he grew older. The feeling could become that of a desperate man and resentment could set in, causing him to cut corners and develop a poor attitude.

The best advice I can give to avoid such feelings is to constantly update your skills. Always be looking out for opportunities to maximize your experience and skills.

If possible, develop a second set of skills or another profession, possibly in the area you really want. It is common these days to drive around and see a bumper sticker proclaiming: "I'd rather be sailing" or "I'd rather be skydiving." If you look closely at people with these kinds of feelings, they may be expressing their frustration for being in a job they don't like, but feel trapped because they feel they can't go forward with what they really would like to be doing.

People who feel trapped in a job can find a way to love their job if they can think back to what attracted them to the job in the first place. If they have a good rapport with their bosses and their colleagues, they can find the sparks again.

Perhaps their best bet is to make an effort to develop skills toward the things they'd really like to be doing and then gradually wean themselves off of their current job. If this is done, they can gently withdraw themselves from the job in which they feel trapped and gradually move towards the job of their dreams.

What this does is give you an option. The option that you know is there for you whenever you decide you want to leave the job you resent and abhor. Yet, you cannot just leave because you have acquired experience and seniority, but more importantly, because you have responsibilities and a lifestyle to maintain.

By far the most important thing you can do is to make note of things you are grateful for in your job. Make a list of people you like, a list of things you like about your job, and show some level of gratitude for having a job when millions are losing theirs or are jobless.

Chapter 2

HOW TO HAVE A POSITIVE ATTITUDE EVEN WHEN YOU DON'T FEEL LIKE IT

It is easier to do a job right than to explain why you didn't.

-Marting Van Buren

In the preceding chapter I suggested that you keep a list of several different things about your job, one of which is a list of things you like or love about your job. It is almost certain that if you don't like your job, it will be a pain in the neck.

It is true that the job will provide you with money – you may even have some prestige and clout on the job, but all of this will be an empty barrel if you don't like your job. In fact, you may find that you avoid identifying yourself with what you do when you introduce yourself to others.

The point is that most of us have a few things we dislike about our jobs.

For example, I used to have a friend who worked as an independent consultant for a seminar company. She enjoyed the training aspect of it but hated the paperwork.

At the same time, I personally love to train and mentor. I derive tremendous satisfaction when I conduct workshops and seminars; and I don't mind paperwork. No matter how tired or ill, once I step onto the platform to speak, the energy level shoots through the roof. Within the first 15 minutes of my session (workshop), I will have referred to over 50% of the participants by their names. (They usually wonder how in the world I manage to remember all that).

With that being said, however, there is one aspect of the trade that I don't like very much and that is having to almost beg or do arm twisting in order to get people to buy books that will help them reinforce their learning.

Even though I like to sell, I feel that in a workshop setting like the one I just described, I don't have to cajole, or preach to people for them to know that these resources would be ideal for them. That it will be a reinforcement of their learning if they will just take the time to read the in depth information I am making available.

My not being very eager to push books is also compounded by the fact that some participants come to the class armed with their assault rifles waiting for the seminar leader to make a pitch or try to sell resources. They will invariably slam him or her in their evaluation.

Some of these things are part of the environment that can create a negative attitude within you without you realizing it. In this case, you allow your environment to control you. Instead, you have to learn to control your environment, so you can build your attitude and get positive results.

That reminds me of my grandmother's admonitions when I was growing up. Each time I displayed a negative attitude or misbehaved, she would come after me with a stick, but I was too fast for her to catch me. As I stated in my Introduction, she would finally say, "You know, having a negative attitude is like going to fish on the river with a leaking fishing boat. You can't have a good fishing experience until you've plugged the hole to stop the leak."

In other words, your attitude is yours. You come up with it and so you have to fix it. You have to adjust it and effect the change you want in order to have a positive experience or else you will become angry and cynical about your job. That can cause you a lot of misery.

No matter who you are, there is a chance there is an aspect of your job that you don't like very much that you will try to avoid. However, the question is: how can you maintain a positive attitude on the job even when you don't feel like it?

Let's play with some ideas to help you develop a positive attitude even when you don't feel like it.

See Work As Play

Dr. Wayne Dyer once said, "When you change the way you look at something, what you're looking at changes." In other words, if you begin to view your work as if you're playing and you can visualize the activities as part of having fun, with time your subconscious mind will begin to believe you and you will begin to relax and enjoy the little pleasures of your work.

The importance of this little exercise is that it will help you reduce stress because you will no longer dread your work. You will no longer see it as work because it becomes part of play. Select all the fun aspects of your work and do them with joy and enthusiasm.

When a truck driver was asked how he could possibly enjoy driving thousands of miles across the country without getting tired, he replied, “It’s all in the attitude. Some truck drivers go to work to drive trucks across the country, but I go for the ride to see the beauty of the country.” To this man, work is play and when you are playing, you are having fun, which invariably gives you a positive attitude about work and life.

Work at Work and Play at Play

Many professionals don’t know how to separate work from play and end up getting in trouble in the process.

In her book titled, *Leader Reach – Essays on the Dynamics of Values, Communication, Spirituality and Power in Leadership,* Dr. Bonnie V. Banks tells the story of a client called Brenda.

Brenda was a workaholic with very little or no interpersonal communication skills. She felt more accomplished while working and had very little time for family and friends. Brenda used to work all day and even brought work home. Very soon, Brenda’s family felt ignored as she became engrossed in her work and continued success. She had little interaction with her staff. She was often seen sending emails or texting a staff member across the hallway instead of walking over to chat. It was all work, work, and more work.

Obviously, Brenda didn't know how to separate work from play. She allowed her work to consume her and left some very important things to fall through the cracks.

People like Brenda may enjoy good fortune and success on the job, but chances are their attitude will be affected with all the pressure to achieve. Therefore, important interpersonal relationships with staff and family suffer leaving people like Brenda impatient and with a negative attitude.

The idea is for you to never allow your work to become your world. Doing so will affect your attitude. Anything that is not part of work will aggravate your already fragile being and you will probably lash out or ignore those causing you problems.

Therefore, work at work, and when you leave your workplace, leave the work there. Don't bring work home. Don't take work on vacation. You may feel like you're important and indispensable, but if you become sick or drop dead, the work will not stop, it will continue.

Never allow yourself to be described as indispensable. If you're ever denied promotion or denied the opportunity to move to another department just because management feels that you're the only one who can do your job, you're in trouble. Nothing can be farther from the truth.

Instead, be a mentor or a leader, and groom people on your team who can step up if and when you're not present to do your job. More about this when we discuss delegation.

Don't allow your work to encroach on your play time, because all work and no play will make your attitude suffer and ruin your chances of upward movement.

Balance your work and play life. Find hobbies and other activities that take you away from work or that can convert what otherwise may be regarded as work into play and fun time for you and your family.

Here's one thing I do in my business:

The most challenging part of my training business is traveling. Running from one airport to another. Flying into a city at night, working all day the following day and then heading out to the airport immediately after my presentation. This hardly gives me time to get to know the city and the people except those I meet in my session or while waiting at the airport.

To break this circle of activities, as a member of Toastmasters International, I seek out clubs within a five- to ten-mile radius of where I'm going and then take time to attend a club meeting on the evening of my arrival. If there is a club that meets in the morning before 7:30, I make plans to attend before going to my workshop.

Because I enjoy speaking in front of audiences, I call ahead to get on the speaking schedule of the clubs I plan to attend. In most cases, I get on their schedules. By the time I get to my main workshop to speak for the next six hours, I'm already pumped up, full of enthusiasm and alert. By this time, my work is no longer work, it's fun!

While waiting at the airport, I write postcards to send back to the people I've met during my trip as well as those I know. This is a reminder to them that I'm still in business and that I still want them to think of me when they need a speaker or trainer. So, I am picking up friends and contacts while doing some marketing along the way.

Your job or business may not involve these types of activities, but you can always find a way to incorporate some fun activities into your job that will add energy to what you do, thereby improving your attitude and getting you excited about work.

Take fun out of what you do and it becomes a chore. Add fun to it and you have something to look forward to every day.

Chapter 3

CHANGING YOUR ATTITUDE TOWARD OTHERS

My father always used to say that when you die, if you've got five real friends, then you've had a great life.

- Lee Iacocca

Having a negative attitude about other people in the work place will no doubt affect your own attitude about your work. When you work with someone you don't really like to see much of, the animosity tends to rub off on your own behavior. This will eventually show up in the way you react or respond to that person. If you happen to be on the same team, chances are your team will suffer, and your team's performance will take a beating as a result of that.

You cannot like everyone and everyone cannot like you. However, to maintain peace of mind, you must have good interpersonal relationships in the workplace. To stay focused on the mission of your team and the organization as a whole, it is important to have a positive attitude toward your colleagues.

Let's face it, you spend at least half of your waking moments at work. How miserable can you be seeing someone you don't want to see? Working alongside someone you don't like or being forced to deal with someone you are not fond of can be disheartening.

However, by looking for the best in this particular person, knowing that you cannot change them, you will save yourself a lot of turmoil and possibly a "Monday morning headache."

No one is absolutely good or absolutely bad. There is usually one thing about a person that is good if you look closely. My point is: if you explore the good side of this person, chances are that he or she will respond favorably and that may be the beginning of a good relationship which will improve the attitude of the person toward you, just as your own attitude toward the person will improve.

Many a time, the attitude you have about others is a reflection of your own personal frustration. At times, it is a reflection of un-met goals and personal failures. It is very easy to point a finger at what others are doing wrong or what they are not doing right. It is what it is, a lame excuse to help us blame others for our shortcomings.

In realty though, when we dig down, we find that we develop negative attitudes toward others because they are not meeting our expectations. When our expectations are not met, we tend to develop our own sullen attitude and become cynical.

Will Rogers once said, "I have never met a man I didn't like." I believe we can all like everyone we meet – to different degrees. Liking people means leaving them feeling good about themselves. Be warm to people even when you don't feel like it. Give people your attention when you are with them and respect their space.

My remedy for changing your negative attitude towards others in the workplace is to focus on the mission of your team and how you and your team can accomplish the mission. Focusing on people tends to bring out the differences which may create personality conflicts.

I recommend that you always look for the best in people. You will inevitably find people who are higher than, lower than, and equal to you. If you concentrate on those features instead of what they can do and what they can contribute, you stand the risk of missing the point.

Chapter 4

SEEING THROUGH YOUR BOSS'S EYES

Don't judge your boss until you have walked a mile in his or her shoes.

- Ola Joseph

Many poor attitudes that most employees develop emanates from the fact that they see their bosses or managers as enemies instead of partners. Bosses have goals to meet in order to make the establishment profitable so that employees can get paid the wages they were promised when they were hired.

On the other hand, employees want to make sure the establishment is profitable so that it can afford to pay the wages it promised to pay.

To this end, both labor and management seem to be heading in the same direction and that should make them partners on the journey. But this is not always the case. According to Douglas McGregor's theory of X and Y, they are not complimentary.

In the X-Theory, McGregor opined in his theory X that an average employee:

- Dislikes work and attempts to avoid it
- Has no ambition, wants no responsibility and would rather follow than lead
- Is self-centered and does not care about organizational goals
- Resists change
- Is gullible and not particularly intelligent
- Assumes people work only for money & security

On the other hand, Theory Y states that to an average employee:

- Work can be as natural as play & rest
- People will be self-directed to meet their work objectives if they are committed to them
- People will be committed to their objectives if rewards are in place that address higher needs such as self-fulfillment
- Under these conditions people will seek responsibility
- Most people can handle responsibility because creativity and ingenuity are common

Without flogging a dead horse, the idea here is (depending on how your boss sees things) that it may be a good idea to look at things from your boss's point of view and know that no matter where he or she is coming from, one thing is certain, and that is to make the company profitable.

Let's explore this area for a moment. What is the "number one" duty of a boss or a manager? Each time I ask this question in a class, I get several answers ranging from "to work with people to get things done," to "motivating employees," to "give directions," to "lead," etc. These answers and anything in between are good, but they are not a manager's number one duty. What then is the manager's number one duty?

The answer to that question is: "To make sure that employees do what they are hired and paid to do." No more, no less. If an employee is not doing what he or she was hired and being paid to do, that employee has no place on the payroll.

After this number one job, everything else in terms of strategy, policy, rules, accommodation, incentive, motivation and/or at times, punishment, are just to help the manager accomplish the number one task of getting the employees to do what they are hired and paid to do.

Working on this premise, therefore, an employee will fare well if he or she can see things from the boss's point of view and know that the boss is not just there to make things difficult or there to see you fail. The boss is there to see you succeed. There may be something wrong in the strategy or the approach, but always remember that the manager cannot do all the work by him or herself. People will be needed to carry out the functions.

When you, the employee, begin to look at things from your manager's point of view, and you begin to think like a manager, see like a manager and act like a manager, you will begin to see why your manager is the way he or she is and why he/she acts a certain way.

One of the best ways to see things from the manager's point of view is to network with your manager and get into his head. Ask questions, show willingness to learn and make your manager feel that you're there to do what you can to help him or her accomplish team goals.

Show an understanding of the manager's situation. See your manager as a partner because both of you want to make sure that the establishment is profitable. Only when the company makes money can you and your manager retain your jobs. Only then can the management be happy and only then can you say you've done what you were hired and paid to do.

As an employee, you must figure your boss out. Is your boss just a boss or is he a mentor-minded boss?

A boss who is just a "boss" sees you (the employee) as one more cog in his machine, another "problem" to deal with on a daily basis. He sees you as someone who does not like work and has to be cajoled or threatened. He sees you as someone who will avoid work if and when it is possible.

If on the other hand you are smart, energetic, and hardworking, your boss, instead of seeing you as a partner, may look at you as a threat. Especially if your boss has what I call the "Mosquito Mentality" whereby he thinks you're there to take his job. That being the case, he will probably see you as someone to keep at bay. He will keep information from you to make sure that doesn't happen.

Unless you understand these facts and look at yourself from your boss's point of view, you will not be able to function and perform your duties.

If, however, you have a boss who is "mentor-minded," who really wants you to succeed by helping you develop your skills, you still have to see yourself or look at things from his or her point of view for you to realize that is what is going on.

A mentor-minded boss will reveal to you all necessary information at his disposal. He will take you under his wing. He will become a friend of yours and help you in several different ways to prepare you for the next level.

A mentor-minded boss is a leader who is trying to groom others to step up when he steps out. He has a vision and would share his vision with you so that at any point in time, you know what he is doing.

A mentor-minded boss usually develops a relationship akin to that of a big-brother or big- sister with you. He will trust you and give you praise whenever you deserve it, correct you whenever you go wrong. He will help you develop a personal and professional goal for both short and long term. A mentor-minded boss doesn't feel threatened by your brilliance or by your ideas. In fact, he welcomes them. A mentor-minded boss will delegate a lot of jobs to you in an attempt to bring you up to speed. He will let you overshadow him on projects so you can learn and grow.

For small-minded employees, it would look like the boss is abdicating his position or that he is piling all the work on you while he is gallivanting around. It is your duty to ask or figure out that what your mentor-minded boss is doing is training (mentoring) you to become a leader so that you too can lead effectively. Once you recognize this, you can begin to soak it in and begin to learn as much as you can. It takes an open-minded employee to see what the mentor-mined boss is doing.

The point is, unless you take a good look at yourself or your activities from your manager's point of view, you may not know why some actions are taken and why things are the way they are at work.

Always keep in mind that the boss has the responsibility to make sure that all the employees are doing what they are hired and paid to do, without which he or she will be out of a job because as Shakespeare once put it,

"Uneasy lies the head that wears the crown." It is, therefore, necessary to see things from the boss's point of view. If your boss is constantly calling on you to work, it is because he trusts you to do a good job. If he delegates assignments to you, it is because he wants you to learn and grow while he frees up his time to concentrate on projects that have more value for him and the organization.

Look closely at your boss and determine what kind of a boss you have and try to work together. No matter what kind of a boss you have, you both have a stake in the organization. Unless the organization is profitable and meets its objectives, both of you may not have a job for very long.

A positive attitude towards your boss, your coworkers, and the organization as a whole will not only help you develop professionally, it will also give you the ability to live a fulfilled life.

Remember, you spend a third or more of your day with your boss at work, you don't want to ruin all that time by displaying a negative attitude. Instead, see your boss as a partner and work together with him or her. If you push your boss up, he will pull you up. If you try to hold him down with a negative attitude, you will remain down with him. This goes for everything in life. When you lift someone up, you rise up with him.

Thcrcforc, always look for the best in your boss and find a way to make life easier for him. Remember, what goes around, comes around. When you give, you also take and whatever you put in your boss's life will come back to you.

Chapter 5

WHEN YOU ARE THE BOSS!

A good boss makes his men realize they have more ability than they think they have so that they consistently do better work than they thought they could.

– Charles Erwin Wilson

Being the boss carries a lot of weight and gives you the opportunity to help not only your company grow but help your employees grow.

When you're the boss, you have only one duty and that duty is to get your employees to do what they are hired to do. In order to perform this task successfully, you must be able to build a solid team. To build a solid team, you must be willing to be a team player and also a leader.

My first hypothetical example here is that of ABC basketball team. There is a very good player on this team who is simply known as "J." Sometimes, this man scores over 60 points in a game and yet his team is defeated by a less qualified team. The reason is not far-fetched. It is because other team members fail to contribute their quota to the team effort.

The point here is that when you are the boss, don't ever try to solve all the problems or try to do everything. You must encourage all employees to contribute to the team effort. Then and only then can you be assured of success for the team.

Having mentioned the example of team player, let us look at some of the areas you must concentrate on to help you do a good job as a boss, which will help you improve the attitude of your team members. That in turn will help improve the services and the products of your company.

Here are three questions you must endeavor to answer:

a) What kind of a boss do I want to be?
b) What can I do to motivate and retain my best employees?
c) What do I need to work on the most?

a) What kind of boss do I want do be?

Leadership skills are very important. Failure to lead effectively will spell disaster for you as a boss. The ability to lead your team will not only improve the morale of the team and foster some good team effort and improve attitude, but will also help dictate where the team will end up and how the team will perform.

To be a good leader, you must be willing to bring your people together and lead by example. Leading by example is doing and participating in activities that you want your team members to take part in.

As a leader, you want to be seen as someone who cares about the team. It is not just about getting the job done; it is about the people. The best thing you can do as a leader is to build relationships with your team members. When you build relationships with your team members, they will feel valued and appreciated, and they will give you their best effort.

In his book *Punished by Rewards*, Alfie Kohn opined, "That people actually do inferior work when enticed with money, rewards and other incentives." In other words, money is not always a motivator to do good work. While people will work harder if they perceive their pay to be unfair, they don't necessarily work harder for more money. The most effective motivational tool is relationship-building.

b) What can I do to motivate and retain my employees?

Having taught and worked with many supervisors, frontline employees and management staff over the years, I strongly believe that the best way to motivate employees is by building relationships.

People are people – they experience the same type of emotional roller-coaster events. They have feelings, they have aspirations, and they have concerns. They have families, needs, and fears.

As a boss or manager, although your number one job is to get the employees to do what they are hired and paid to do, you will also be playing a major role in their lives. If you want every employee to give you his best effort, you, the boss have to look for the best in every employee. If you want every employee to have a positive attitude, you have to find a way to build relationships with every employee. Every employee must see you as a caring boss.

Employees don't care how much you know, but they want a leader who cares about them. A boss they can trust and depend upon. When they discover you are that kind of a leader or boss, their morale and attitude will take on a positive tone. When an employee is rewarded or recognized for displaying a positive attitude, others will emulate him and that will spread the positive vibes like ripples in the water.

When you are the boss, build relationships with your employees, communicate with them, show them you care, treat them with respect, lead by example, and they will be inspired and motivated to want to work with and for you.

If you treat them like robots, you will find it difficult to hold on to them, especially the good ones. They will be very quick to take their skills and knowledge elsewhere.

Always remember that people will forget what you say. They will forget what you do. But they will never forget how you make them feel. It's all in the attitude.

c) What do I need to work on the most?

Every boss or leader, no matter how good, can find something to improve. An effective boss is both a manager and a leader. However, leadership skills are the ones that will really elevate you and raise your visibility.

To be more effective as a leader, here are a few things to work on:

- **Set goals with your employees**: People work better and smarter when they know exactly what is expected of them and they know where they are going. A goal will give them a roadmap and when they arrive at their destination, they will recognize it.
- **Communicate willingly**: The number one complaint employees and team members have is that they don't know what is going on because no one is communicating with them. As a manager you want to have an open line of communication with your employees. Open communication will help you build a good relationship with your team. Remember, their work is their life. It is where they feel secure. If they don't know what is going on, then their sense of security is threatened and a negative attitude may set in.
- **Keep learning**: Never consider yourself as knowledgeable enough to the extent that you stop learning. Keep learning, keep improving yourself especially with modern technology so that you can be ahead of the game. While you are not supposed

to solve all problems, you have to been seen as the "go to" person.

- **Be a change agent**: Be flexible and ready to accept change. Rigidity and dogmatism will hinder your ability to lead effectively. Negative attitude towards change can have a negative impact on your team and the organization as a whole. Be prepared to embrace change as soon as you find out that it is necessary. Never drag your feet or hesitate when it comes to embracing change.
- **Acknowledge employee accomplishments**: Nothing creates more problems for a manager or a leader than the failure to acknowledge employee accomplishments. Never take credit for what the employees have done. Unappreciated workforce is a disgruntled workforce and nothing good can come out of such a team. In fact, some of the brilliant members of the team will soon become "flight risks" or begin to jump ship if they sense that their efforts are not appreciated by the leadership. Recognize team accomplishments and reward team members. Give feedback constantly and praise people for a job well done.

Chapter 6

STAYING AFLOAT IN A SEA OF CONSTANT CHANGE

Change is inevitable, except from a vending machine.

- Bumper Sticker

One of the things that get on the nerves of employees and affect their Attitude at work is change. Most people do not naturally like change. Even when they don't like the status quo, they prefer to deal with the devil they know rather than the angel they don't know.

Change has been known to create fear in the minds of workers over the years, especially if management fails to explain the reason for the change and/or what the people stand to gain as a result of the change.

It is natural for employees to view change as a ploy by the management to either cut back on resources, reduce workforce or as an attempt to take away employees' privileges. Therefore, employees tend to view change with suspicion. Even when the reason for change is communicated, the tendency is for employees to take the explanation with a grain of salt.

The number one antidote for the fear of change experienced by employees is for the management to begin to communicate the impending change well ahead of time. There must be an open communication of why the change is necessary, when it is coming, how it is going to come, who will bring the change, who will be affected and what it will mean to the workers. Most importantly, what's in it for the people or what do they stand to gain as a result of the change?

The above-mentioned points are so critical that if they are not communicated, people will begin to fabricate their own reasons, and rumors will begin to fly. Once that starts, it makes it difficult for management to initiate the change, and that makes it more difficult for the people to sort out what is true from what is not.

A good example was the recent Health Care debate in the United States Congress. Because the White House was (perceived to be) too slow to address a lot of the misconceptions put out by those opposing revamping of the Health Care bill, rumors began to fly, such as, "it is an attempt or a ploy to kill elderly people," "it will take away Medicare benefits from seniors," or "it will be used to pay for abortions" or "it is socialist medicine and there is going to be an Armageddon if it passes," etc.

By the time the White House began to step in to correct the misconceptions, tempers had started flying, opponents had gained traction. People were confused because they couldn't figure out what was real and what was not.

The bill eventually passed on the floor of the House on Sunday, March 21, 2010, and was signed into law by President Obama on Tuesday, March 23, 2010.

The lesson here is to begin to communicate what you want people to know aggressively before rumors take a foothold or gain traction because once that happens, you will need to spend extra time and effort to correct the misconception put out by those who do not want to see the measure succeed or by your detractors.

The question then is how does an employee deal with change?

The first thing you can do as an employee is to be flexible and be willing to accept change or be prepared to be left behind.

Change is constant! The fact is that whether you know it or not, change is taking place every nanosecond of the day.

Two Things To Watch for When It Comes To Staying Afloat In The Sea Of Change

As an employee, there are two things to watch out for when it comes to staying afloat in the sea of change. These are your 1) habit; and 2) attitude towards change.

Habit

The first of the two change inhibitors in employees is **habit**.

To demonstrate how change may cause discomfort and, therefore, resistance, let's look at what leads to resistance to change in the first place.

I was speaking at a national convention in Florida a few years ago when I decided to play a game made popular by John Newstrom and Edward Scannell in their book, *Games Trainers Play,* which shows two exercises that highlight the power of habit over human beings and how we resist change.

I asked the audience to simply clasp their hands with their fingers interlocked in a prayerful fashion. I then asked them to glance down at their hands and fingers to see how their thumbs and fingers were interlocked.

"Pull your hands apart and re-clasp them in the opposite way" (i.e., if your left thumb was below the right one initially, the right thumb would now be on top).

Even before I asked them how they felt, people were shaking their heads and rolling their eyes.

"Now see if you feel comfortable in this position," I said to them.

A woman shouted out, "This is weird." Another one said, "It is strange." "It is very uncomfortable," said yet another member of the audience.

For some people, this physical change presents no problem, but for most people even this minor physical change causes discomfort and makes them feel awkward, uncomfortable and out of balance.

Here is another exercise:

Effect of Habit on Change

1) I	2) _ _ _ _ _

Now place a dot on the "I"

Write the word "XEROX" in the spaces provided in box

Answer 1: Did you place your dot on the I or did you dot your I? If you dotted your "I", you are wrong because the letter is a capital letter and need not be dotted. Instead the dot should be placed on it.

Answer 2: The word should be written in the spaces not on the broken lines.

Here is where the habit comes in. All your life you've been told to dot your I's and cross your T's and that's what you do naturally. On the second one, you are used to writing on dotted lines rather than in between the lines.

The foregoing exercises show that we create a habit over a period of time and we become so comfortable that breaking such a habit becomes a problem and making a change becomes difficult. Our resistance to change comes from our old habits.

Some people go through all kinds of roller-coaster emotions whenever they experience some change in their lives ranging from elation to being scared and paranoid.

I received the following from John Di Lemme, a good friend of mine, during a visit to Atlanta, and I feel it is the best definition of habit I have read:

I'm your constant companion
I'm your greatest helper or your heaviest burden.
I will push you onward or drag you down to failure
I'm completely at your command.
Half the things you do, you might just as well turn over to me,
And I will be able to do them quickly and correctly.
I'm easily managed; you must merely be firm with me.
Show me exactly how you want something done, and after a few lessons I will do it automatically.
I'm the servant of all great men.
And, alas, of all failures as well.
Those who are great, I have made great.
Those who are failures, I have made failures.
I'm not a machine, though I work with all the precision of a machine.
Plus, the intelligence of a man.
You may run me for profit, or run me for ruin; it makes no difference to me.
Take me, train me, be firm with me and I will put the world

at you feet.
Be easy with me, and I will destroy you.
Who am I?
I'm a HABIT!

We've all experienced the dread and the agony of change. Whether at work, at home or even in the community. Be it leaving home for school for the first time, showing up for work on the first day or having a new baby in the family. It is certain that all what we dread and the emotional roller coaster we experienced is because of our resistance to change.

Most of us go through the same routine on a daily basis. We wake up in the morning and follow the same routine. We do the same set of activities in the same sequence. We go to work driving the same route. We tend to carry out these activities mechanically.

Some of us have thousands of restaurants in our cities, but we eat in the same restaurant all year round. These are signs of habits created over the years.

In Houston where I live, there are four Sam's Clubs within a ten-mile radius of my house.

For years, I have consistently shopped in just one of them. Out of habit, I know my way around this one location so well that I can be in and out in less than 10 minutes depending on what I want to buy. I know the employees there and they know me, some on a first name basis.

However, each time I ventured into any of the other three stores, I couldn't seem to find my way around, let alone find what I was looking for. Most of the time, when I came out of the store, I had to stop to gather my thoughts to find my bearings. Consequently, I ended up wasting time and energy just wandering around.

One day, I felt so frustrated that I left the shopping cart in the aisle, walked out and drove to the one location I was familiar with.

For several years, I resisted the urge to become familiar with the other new locations.

That is what habit does to you. It forces you to become so comfortable that you become afraid to change. Some people are so scared of change that just the mere mention of it sends them diving for cover.

But, you see, it doesn't have to be that way.

When you realize that we live in a changing world, and that things are constantly changing, you will see that it doesn't matter whether you dread it or not, change will come anyway.

In fact, it is a common saying that the only constant thing in life is change.

The fact is that most people are afraid of change because they are afraid to change their habits. That is why habit is a strong change inhibitor. Habit makes you feel comfortable and prevents you from making a change that is necessary to make your life better.

Attitude

The second change inhibitor in employees is their attitude towards their job, their colleagues, the management, and the company.

It is about how you feel about change and how you react or respond to it. Your attitude to change eventually affects how you behave towards your family, your friends, your job, and many other aspects of your life.

Your responses or reactions to change usually have profound effects on your life. Flexibility and adaptability can be very rewarding if properly applied at the right time and place.

In other words, sometimes a change of attitude is all you need to make things better.

My suggestion to you is hang in there if what you're doing makes sense, but don't be afraid to make a change when it is necessary.

I know some of us contend with the idea to remain strong and firm.

I recognize the fact that we have to be strong and firm, but the question is why struggle against the current if a change is necessary?

When you find yourselves in a position where you need to be flexible, you must change or adapt to the situation whether you're forced into it or you cause it to happen. Otherwise, you will be left behind.

When a change is introduced, those who like it and are flexible enough to embrace it usually glide along smoothly and effortlessly.

On the other hand, those who resist it normally have difficulty coping with it and this creates a stressful situation for them and those around them.

Often times those who resist change become very cynical and pessimistic. If something should go wrong, they are quick to point it out and blame it on the change that was made. The big question though is, why is it that people fear change?

I recently spoke to a group of people at a conference and I asked them to tell me what helps people achieve success. Most of them chose hard work, some chose commitment while others chose loyalty. Then I made them do the following exercise.

I had them write the alphabet A - Z (vertically) and then place the corresponding numbers, e.g. A=1, B=2, C=3 etc.

1 = A
2 = B
3 = C
4 = D
5 = E
6 = F
7 = G
8 = H
9 = I
10 = J
11 = K
12 = L
13 = M
14 = N
15 = O
16 = P
17 = Q

18 = R
19 = S
20 = T
21 = U
22 = V
23 – W
24 = X
25 = Y
26 = Z

Then I asked them to write the word **"HARDWORK"** (vertically) and write the corresponding number to each letter as it appears on the alphabet:

H	**A**	**R**	**D**	**W**	**O**	**R**	**K**	
8	**1**	**18**	**4**	**23**	**15**	**18**	**11**	**= 98**

We then wrote out the word **ATTITUDE** (vertically) and the corresponding number to each letter as it appears on the alphabet.

A	**T**	**T**	**I**	**T**	**U**	**D**	**E**	
1	**20**	**20**	**9**	**20**	**21**	**4**	**5**	**= 100**

At the end of this exercise, it became clear to the audience that hard work alone cannot bring the necessary success and change unless it is accompanied by positive attitude towards change.

Not only that, if you look closely, you will notice that the letter **"U"** has the highest score. The letter **"U"** is used here to represent "**YOU**." This simply means that the change must start with you.

Charles Swindoll, an American pastor was once quoted as saying, "Attitude is more important than facts. It is more important than the past, than education, than money, than circumstances, than failures, than success, than what other people think, say or do. It will break a company, a church, a home."

"The remarkable thing is you have a choice every day regarding the attitude you will embrace for that day. We cannot change our past…you cannot change the fact that people will act in a certain way. You cannot change the inevitable. The only thing you can change is you and your attitude."

The point, therefore, is that if there is going to be any notable change, there must be a change of attitude and that change of attitude must start with you.

As Dr. Wayne Dyer would say, "When you change your attitude about the thing you are looking at, what you are looking at also changes."

Negative attitude is a major change inhibitor. Unless you are willing to change your attitude, you will not be in a position to effect a change.

In an article by Gretchin William-Morris in the *Texas Southern University Herald*, a story was told by a man who several years ago was asked to give a commencement address. After he had given his speech, he sat down to watch the graduates receive their college degrees. Suddenly, the entire audience began applauding for a student who had earned a perfect 4.0 GPA. During the applause, a faculty member seated next to the speaker leaned over and said to him, "She may be a Miss Genius, but her attitude stinks." The speaker later said, "Without even thinking, my hands stopped clapping in mid-air. I couldn't help but think, how sad!"

You cannot become what you need to be, whilst remaining what you are. A change of attitude can be the difference between success and failure. Take care of your attitude and you will go places. "Hardwork" cannot give you 100% results, however, a great “Attitude” can give you 100% results and more.

Attitude is contagious! Make sure you are catching the right one!

Chapter 7

HOW YOUR APPEARANCE AFFECTS YOUR ATTITUDE

Keeping your clothes well pressed will keep you from looking hard pressed.

- Coleman Cox

You may not realize it but your attitude has a lot to do with your appearance. In fact, just like your appearance says a lot about you, it also affects your attitude for better or for worse.

Studies have shown that a person who is properly and comfortably dressed is likely to project a positive attitude because he or she feels good with him/herself.

Appearance doesn't have to be expensive or flamboyant; it just needs to be appropriate, acceptable and comfortable, and not distracting to clients or colleagues at work. One that does not project an image of "I don't care how I look" or "I don't care what you think" is likely to engender poor attitude.

I once watched a makeover program on TV where a group of poorly dressed women were featured. Many of these women were quite lovely, but because of their jobs and caring for their families, they allowed themselves to fall behind in their appearance. Some had been going around for years in faded, worn-out jeans and baggy sweaters or T-shirts. Their hair tied in a pony-tail or left unkempt. The only person they were attractive to were their husbands, who themselves were disheveled because they too had taken the attitude of "who cares?"

On the program, their "before" photos were on display for all to see while the makeover group was working on improving the appearance of the participants.

After the transformation, the women did not recognize themselves. One actually asked, "Who's that in that photo? That's not me," she said. All the women became instant beauties. They were more attractive, more beautiful, and had an air of confidence and "can do" attitudes about them.

This is also true about the way you appear at work. To enhance your Attitude At Work, I recommend that you dress appropriately and comfortably. When you are properly and comfortably dressed for work, you exude confidence and project a positive attitude. People will find you approachable.

If you wear a uniform, keep your uniform looking clean, neat and pressed. Make sure you get the proper size and wear it with pride.

When I was in the military, I spent countless hours taking care of my uniforms just like other sailors. I was very particular about my white uniforms, so I did the laundry personally because I didn't think the dry cleaners could do it the way I wanted. I had a secret substance from Nigeria I applied to my white uniforms that made them look brand new. My shipmates were always surprised to see me get the best dressed sailor's award at the personnel inspection parade every week. They had no clue what was going on or what I was doing.

It wasn't that the other sailors' uniforms were not "squared away," it was just the little extra care given to my uniform that made a big difference.

This undoubtedly affected my positive attitude as I was always looking forward to our weekly personnel inspection. I was confident in wearing my uniform everywhere because it looked good on me and was well taken-care of.

To know why I was so fascinated about taking care of my white uniform, you would have to go back to my high school days in Nigeria where our uniform was white pants and white shirt. We had to keep them sparkling.

When not wearing a uniform, you have a better chance of positively affecting your appearance. Your choice of colors can be coordinated in such a way that you appear clean and appropriately dressed at all times.

Color coordination is important when you want to dress well. Women have more choices than men in this regard depending on their industry or profession.

To learn more about appearance, I highly recommend that you read John T. Molloy's book *New Dress For Success*. Whatever your taste, you will find something for you.

Personally, my favorite color combination is Navy Blue trousers (pants) and white shirt. In fact, I could dress myself in those colors all year-round without getting tired of them. Most men look good in that color combination as well.

Wearing my favorite color combination has a way of affecting my attitude. I feel good inside out. I'm upbeat.

In fact, whenever I'm appropriately dressed in my favorite colors, I feel exceptionally happy and cheerful – even when I have no money in my pocket or in my bank account.

You must also remember that people draw conclusions and judge you within 30 seconds of seeing you based on your appearance. It is not fair, but that is the reality.

Here is an example: On the first day of a new school year, a young female professor went into the lecture room and sat in the front row. Her appearance did not say anything about who she was. In fact, she could have easily passed for one of the students.

As the students walked in, some nodded to acknowledge her while some just walked past her without making eye contact.

When it was time for the class to begin, she stood up, walked to the front of the class and wrote on the board that every student should write their opinion about her on a piece of paper. Just anything. Whatever they thought of her.

They did!

The funny part of this exercise was that, even though the students had not formally met her, they didn't know her name (except for what they had on their schedule). They didn't even know if she was the person whose name was on their schedule.

Needless to say, most of what was written was based on the students' perception which was based on the professor's appearance.

I have had several experiences of this kind of judgment or what I call mistaken identity.

A few years ago, I was at the Veterans Affairs Medical Center in Houston to see my doctor. As I walked in, there were three women in the nurses' room talking. Two of them were standing with their backs to the door while one was facing the door. As soon as I came into her view she screamed, "Oh Lord, here comes the pastor!"

I turned at the same time as the other two women turned, looking behind me to see who was there, but she said, "No sir, it is you. You are a pastor, aren't you?" "No," I murmured, pleasantly surprised.

"It is written all over you, sir," she insisted.

"I'm not a pastor, but what the pastors do on the pulpit, I do on the platform," I said. "I'm a professional speaker." The other two women just stood looking at me wide eyed.

The women eventually got me to visit and speak at their church events because one of them was the wife of a pastor of a small church. I was also invited to speak at their weekly fellowship service at the Veterans Affairs Medical Center in Houston.

A similar thing happened one day at the courthouse. I was in Small Claims Court waiting for the proceedings to begin.

The clerk came in and whispered to the Deputy to have me move to the front area reserved for attorneys. I told him I was not a lawyer.

Not long after, the judge came in. We all stood as she was announced. She sat down, asked the people to please sit, then conferred with her staff. She looked out at the courtroom, spotted me and thought I was an attorney. She looked at me and said, "Counsel, please take your seat here (pointing to the front row). I had to stand up to say I was not a lawyer. She laughed, and apologized for her mistake. Humored, she asked: “Why did you come in here looking like an attorney?” To which I responded, “Maybe I should have been one, your honor.” We all laughed.

On another occasion I had gone to the courthouse to renew my vehicle registration. As I came out a woman ran after me saying, “Excuse me sir, excuse me sir.” I was walking so fast that she had to chase me down in the parking lot. When I realized she was calling me I turned and asked how I could help her.

She said she needed an attorney. I almost burst out laughing, but I managed to maintain a straight face as I asked her why.

After she explained her problem I told her that she didn’t need an attorney to do what she needed to do. All she really needed was to obtain the form, fill it out, notarize it and submit it with her fees.

These are examples to let you see how people judge you and draw conclusions about you even before they know who you are. I have been mistaken for a doctor, I have been mistaken for a professor. Many times I have been approached inside department stores because people thought I was one of the salesmen due to the way I dressed. In short, I see this a lot.

At times I almost have to apologize for misleading people, but it is all due to the way I dress: shirt, tie and most often with my blazer on.

I highly recommend that whatever you do, dress appropriately. It will have a great impact on your attitude. It is better to be a little overdressed than to be underdressed. Better to be mistaken for an attorney and be treated as one than to be mistaken for a janitor and be asked to clean up a spill on the floor.

I don't have a PhD, I have never introduced myself as a Dr. or a PhD, yet people would get on the platform to introduce me and they would introduce me as Dr. Joseph. In fact, at a conference where I was scheduled to speak, I got to the auditorium only to find a life-size poster of me. Of course I was called "Dr." Ola Joseph. My name badge was "Dr." and the table card bore Dr. Ola Joseph.

Although I don't condone these mistakes and I don't present myself as a Dr. or PhD holder, it is pleasant when people just assume I'm what I'm not. Of course, it is better than to be presumed to be something else.

If you want to improve your attitude, be treated with respect and be acknowledged, dress appropriately.

As people in my village would say, "Irinisi ni isonilojo," which simply translates into "you judge people the way you see them."

What does your appearance say about you?

Chapter 8

DELEGATE YOUR WAY TO SUCCESS?

Don't do anything that someone else can do for you.

- Bill Marriott, Sr.

In order to cultivate positive Attitude At Work, you must use all the resources at your disposal. If you are a manager or a leader, you must use the talents of your people to get the job done. This you can accomplish by effectively delegating work to all your team members. That's why you hire them.

Even if you are not the boss (which means you don't have the luxury of delegating assignments to others), you can negotiate in order to make sure that you are not buried under a pile of work while other team members have less or nothing to do.

Negotiation is a situation whereby you can help your boss prioritize to make sure that first things get done first. When you are busy doing something for your boss, and he has forgotten that you are working on another task, just simply ask if he wants you to suspend work on the project at hand and go on to something else. You should ask your boss which of the tasks he wants you to do first.

Using the principle of delegation effectively can help you as a team leader get a lot done in order to accomplish your number one objective as a supervisor in the workplace.

The basic principle here is that when you delegate assignments to your team members, you are getting everyone involved in the team effort, and everyone is making contributions to the growth of the organization.

Why is it important to delegate?

It is important to delegate because failure to delegate assignments means that you, the leader, will be doing most of the work, if not all of it. It probably shows that you are the only one who knows what to do and when, for some reason, you are not present, nothing gets done.

As I pointed out before, whether you're a leader or a member of the team, don't be the only one with the solution. Never solve all the problems. Instead make sure that everyone has access to the information so that when you are not present, someone else can step up and take charge. If you are the only one who knows what to do, you are not a good leader, and you are not a good team player. It means that without you the team is stuck, and when you can't perform, your team becomes another team that cannot win a game without its star player.

What Delegation Will Do For You

When you delegate work to other team members, you make them earn their pay. You give them a sense of being worthy players and a sense of pride at what they do. Here are some of the things employing this principle will do for you, your team, and your organization.

- Delegating work to other team members or employees will allow the manager/leader to spend time on projects that brings the most value to the organization.
- It helps to divide work among team members so that no single team member is overworked or left without something to do.
- This will also help to increase employee commitment to the company. They have something at stake.
- Delegation helps to develop team members, prepare them to lead, and become effective leaders or supervisors.

- When you delegate it frees up your time. You will not work overtime that you don't get paid for and you will not have to take work home.
- It helps to reduce cost of operation as people learn on the job. If well-implemented employees or team members get cross-trained in other people's functions, that reduces the cost of training the employees in those areas.

Remember to help your team members grow by delegating assignments to them. Don't hold your team for ransom when you are not available simply because you are the only one who has the answer or knows what to do.

Give them work to do. Utilize their skills. Isn't that why you hire them?

Chapter 9

HOW TO MAKE YOUR BOSS LOOK GOOD

Being the boss anywhere is lonely. Being a female boss in a world of mostly men is especially so.

- Robert Frost

Making your boss look good through positive attitude is a good way to help you love and keep your job. When you maintain a good attitude at work, you are not only making things easier for yourself, you are also helping to make your boss look good. In return you get a good review, a pay raise and most of all, peace of mind and satisfaction that you've given your best effort for the day's job.

I learned this important lesson a few years ago when I enlisted in the United States Navy. What happened at this event taught me a very important lesson on how to use discretion, good judgment, and going the extra mile while making others look good. It does have its rewards.

I had just completed my basic training at the Naval Training Center (NTC) in San Diego. After a brief stint at NTC, I was deployed to my first duty station at the

Submarine Base, Point Loma, which was a few miles down the street from the NTC.

Unknown to me at the time, my boss at NTC didn't want to release me. He requested that I be retained at NTC, but the Navy refused. Of course I had no idea that something like that was going on behind the scenes. I was among the last sailors among my shipmates to leave the NTC.

Eventually I got my transfer orders and proceeded to the Submarine Base (Subase) in Point Loma, San Diego.

When I showed up at Subase, I was warmly welcomed. I didn't know my way around, but I was not concerned since I had no pressing matters. All I needed to know for now was the location of the library. I was shown my desk, but did not have a specific assignment.

I did not have an office key or computer password. I had to wait for someone to open the door every morning for the first two weeks. In fact, I was beginning to feel like I was not wanted there because I had nothing to do other than distribute mail. In short, I didn't know what to do, but I kept my ears and eyes open. I tried to take in as much as I could while trying to understand the operation of the new place. I wasn't used to just sitting around, so I poured my energy into reading, spending every free moment in the library.

Two-and-a-half weeks after reporting to the station, I overheard the Command Master Chief and my Senior Chief talking about sailors in the barracks who had not paid their phone bills. Some owed several hundred dollars, and the commander had no money to keep paying the bills on behalf of the sailors, many of whom were out on six-month deployments.

Later I saw my boss and other officers looking at some computer printouts. I overheard them discussing tabulating the info to know who owed what and for how long. The Command Master Chief told my boss to investigate and get back to him because the Commanding Officer (CO) wanted to know. After they left, I did my own investigation to get an idea of what was going on.

After a few minutes I began to understand the problems due to my ability to understand tabulated reports. But I had not been asked to do it. I wasn't even sure my Senior Chief knew I could type.

Every time I was alone in the office, I would open the binders containing the computer printouts to try and figure out a way to do the report based on what I overheard them saying.

The following week, I got what I wanted. I got a key to the office and since I lived on base, it was not difficult for me to come and go. For a few days I kept looking at the computer printouts, studying them and figuring out several ways of doing it.

Then Friday came, and everyone left to go home. I came back to the office and carried all the computer printouts to my barracks. I started pouring over them; looking for names of sailors, their different commands, how much they owed and for how long.

Soon, it became clear what I needed to do to get the report tabulated.

I started typing and tabulating the report on Friday night. I worked all night, all day Saturday and Sunday. By the time I finished, I had over 1,000 names from more than eight different commands. I had prepared the reports showing who owed what for 30 days, 60 days, 90 days, 120 days, and 180 days.

By 1:00 a.m. that Monday morning, I started printing the reports. I had over 500 pages. In fact, I had to go down to the office in the middle of the night to get more paper because I had used up my own supply. By 4:00 a.m. I finished printing and rushed downstairs to place the reports on my Senior Chief's desk along with the computer printouts. I went back to my room to catch one hour sleep that was much needed.

My boss arrived in the office around 5:00 a.m. He said he didn't have to look far to know who came to the office to do the report. He later told everyone at the Monday morning muster.

After studying the report, he took it to the hill to the Command Master Chief's office who then came with him to our office to compare the report with the computer printouts. Later, the Commanding Officer joined them.

I thought I had a good idea what might happen that morning and I felt good about what I had done, but I wasn't prepared for what happened. I wasn't sure if it was planned or spontaneous, but despite the fact, I was happy at what did happen and I was shocked.

The fact that I had done something good and I knew it, made me feel happy and excited. Although, I had only had just about two hours sleep, my energy level was high as I prepared for work. I left my 4th floor barracks room and went downstairs.

As soon as the elevator doors opened I found my Commanding Officer, Command Master Chief and my Senior Chief standing there as if they were waiting for me. I froze. My mouth ran dry. I was so shocked that for a moment, I forgot I had to salute.

I quickly saluted the CO just as my boss was saying, "That's him Sir. No one else could have done it but him."

"Good job, son! You got us squared away," said the CO. I was tongue-tied. I didn't know what to say. I had only seen him a few times from afar, but never at close range. He had never addressed me directly. He reached to shake my hand, something very uncommon. His big hand enveloped my tiny little hand. As he pumped my hand, he said, "Sailors like you have a great future in my Navy."

I mouthed my thanks and dashed into the office which was just a few yards away, still shaking from the sudden encounter.

That day, my boss had the second bed in my room removed so I could have a private room. I had free cable TV and I had time to go to school. Many a time my boss would come in and ask, "What else do you have for today?"

"Nothing sir," I would reply.

"Do you have classes today?"

"Yes sir."

"Ok, you can go. See you in the morning."

With that one single discretion of getting my boss out of a mess, I had a wonderful experience all throughout my stay at the duty station. Many a time, I was allowed to take a few days off without using my vacation time.

The point here is that when you make your boss look good by going the extra mile and by doing things right even before you are asked, you stand to reap a good reward.

Do you want to get the best out of your boss? Go the extra mile because the traffic is lighter over there and your attitude will greatly improve your chances of getting ahead. Even if you get no pay raise, chances are you will feel happy within.

Learn How To Present Your Ideas Clearly

Many professionals are brilliant and have bright ideas but many don't know how to present their ideas and so they don't share them.

The ability to present your ideas clearly is very important. It can help accelerate your upward movement and provide recognition for awards in the workplace.

The first step toward presenting your idea clearly is to know what you are talking about. This you can do by researching your facts and figures, and be clear about what needs to be communicated to your audience.

The other important skill that you must have in order to present your ideas clearly is to acquire public speaking skills.

Public speaking skills have become an invaluable talent to have in the last few years. In fact, most companies started emphasizing this skill on their job application forms several years ago by asking, "What skills do you have? Name other skills, e.g. public speaking."

People with this important ability are usually very successful in their profession; they are visible and confident. When they speak, people listen to them because they know what they are talking about, and they know how to get their message across to the audience.

My first line of action is to recommend that you go and visit your local Toastmasters Club. There is a club within a five-mile radius of your home or workplace in most big cities in America. Once you join the club, begin to take advantage of the programs to improve your leadership and communication skills. You will use these skills not only at work but with other life endeavors as well.

Also, follow the news and be knowledgeable of current events in your industry as well as other areas. This will allow you to be current and have fresh ideas to present each time you have something to say.

I can almost guarantee you that armed with good public speaking skills, which allow you to present your ideas clearly, and current knowledge of the activities in your industry or your profession, your attitude will be greatly improved and you will love your job.

Be Prepared

The Boys Scouts of America motto is, "Be Prepared." This does not only apply to the scouts, it is also a good motto for professionals.

Being prepared will help you improve yourself and will help your boss look good. This you can do by learning and knowing as much as possible about your job and that of your boss. When you have understudied your boss and you know as much as he does, it will be easy for him to delegate assignments to you while he goes on to other tasks, which will bring more value to your company.

I was delivering a presentation to the administrative staff of Texas A & M University a while back. One of the participants shared her story. She had been in the department for several years. "I knew the department like the back of my hand," she said. When her boss left, the university tried to recruit someone from outside to take the position. She was able to apply and although there were some dissenting voices, she eventually got the job. She was able to prove that she knew the job and was very suitable for it. She had what was required to do a good job as she had been doing that even before the boss left, and she had the support of all the other members of the department.

They had also shown their indignation at the idea of bringing in an outsider to be boss when one of their own could handle the position.

The main reason she was able to get the position is because she was prepared. She met the criteria for the position.

To make yourself more valuable for your boss and your organization, get all the necessary knowledge and qualifications you can get. Then prepare yourself for an opportunity to step up to the plate when the time arrives.

Compliment Your Boss's Good Work

Many employees don't think their bosses need encouragement or a pat on the back for a job well done. But they do.

Bosses are humans. They have a lot riding on them. They get the heat from both ends. The upper management comes down on them asking them to do a lot with fewer and fewer resources. The employees expect them to perform miracles in getting them pay raises, problem solving, and motivating them as well as resolving conflicts. All these increase the stress level of managers and leaders.

At every opportunity, compliment your leader for a job well-done. He will appreciate that.

Some employees don't think it is okay to compliment the boss. One man said, "It is like you are sucking up to the boss." A woman said, "It is likely to be misinterpreted and you could open yourself up to a lawsuit."

Yes, both of those statements are correct. Our society has become so sensitive to little things that the workplace has become a rigid environment where people are no longer expected to express emotions of any kind without someone reading the wrong meaning into them.

However, I think moderation is the key word here. If your compliments are timely, straight to the point and moderately done, it may raise eyebrows but that's all it will do. It will, however, leave your boss feeling good about him or herself. Knowing that someone appreciates their good work.

Never let what you cannot do stop you from doing what you can. Do what you want to do and leave others to talk about it. If your boss does a good job, compliment him just like you would expect him or her to compliment you and write you a good performance review. It helps to build a good working relationship that is conducive to the environment. More importantly, it helps to reduce stress in the workplace.

What goes around comes around. One day you too will become the boss. So apply the golden rule. How would you like to be treated as a boss? Would you like your good work to go unnoticed by your team members, or would you like to be complimented and recognized? Think about it.

Chapter 10

HOW TO GET RECOGNITION FOR YOUR ACCOMPLISHMENTS

Every accomplishment starts with the decision to try. Talking about it is reliving it.

- Ola Joseph

My father used to say, “If you don’t blow your trumpet, someone will use it as a sputum.” This simple statement underlines the fact that if you don’t tell your own story, no one would tell it for you. If you don’t sing your own song, no one would sing it for you.

As an employee, you must learn to sing your own praise and talk about your accomplishments in order for upper management to know. If you rely solely on the fact that someone will notice you, you will be left behind.

One of the reasons most people fail to sing their own praises is their lack of public speaking skills and the fact that a lot of people think talking about themselves is akin to boasting. Some people think it is boasting if they talk about their accomplishments. This is really not true. As an old sage once said, “If you’ve done it, it is not boasting.”

When you have accomplished any feat either personally or professionally, it is appropriate to talk about it and let people know that you have such skills just in case they need someone with your ability.

To accomplish this, learn to speak effectively before audiences. Go to your local Toastmasters Club and learn the art of public speaking. Acquiring public speaking skills will not only help you talk about your own skills, it will also help you become a better communicator.

I highly encourage all employees, junior and senior, to polish their public speaking skills in order to improve themselves personally and professionally. It also has a way of improving attitude tremendously. When an employee can effectively express him or herself, there is the tendency to want to take on leadership roles and get things done timely. Less time is wasted on things that are not very important. Learning to communicate effectively is a skill that all employees must strive to attain.

Other than acquiring public speaking skills, there are other areas where that can help you gain recognition and get rewarded for your accomplishments.

Publish in the company newsletter

Most companies have newsletters that get distributed throughout the company and sometime to outside readers through systematic distribution – or just by an employee taking a copy home for others to read. This is a great way to express yourself as an employee and to make a contribution to the company's profile.

A few years ago I was conducting a workshop in Dallas, Texas, when I met a young man who told me about his experience in this area.

He was a newly-hired employee. Not long after he came on board, he noticed an article in the company's newsletter about an issue that was going on and creating problems to the point of embarrassment for the company.

Not knowing what to do or how to make his voice heard since he was a junior employee, he decided to contribute an article to the next edition of the newsletter. He wrote a rejoinder to the article highlighting what he considered the highpoints and the low points. He proffered some solutions of his own and made suggestions on how to handle others.

The president of the company read the rejoinder written by the young man. He called the new employee into his office and praised his ideas which proved to be very good for the company.

The end result was that a unit was created and the young man was made the head of the unit in addition to his duties. He was a one-man unit and reported directly to the president. Needless to say, he was excited and loved his job. It was clear from the way he felt while talking to me that he was very happy. He was handsomely rewarded for his contribution.

It is a good strategy to share your ideas at work through writing. You never know who is looking, reading or listening. Your idea may be just what the company needs to get out of a slump, but if you fail to share your ideas, the company will be robbed of such a resource.

Community Events

Another attitude booster at work is brought about by taking part in community events. Many companies engage in activities in their communities, and it is a great way to give back to the community. It is also a good way to boost employee morale and improve the attitude of those who participate. No wonder companies encourage their employees to take part in community activities as well as match employee donations to charities.

There is something satisfying about volunteering at community events. The feeling that you are making a difference in someone's life is gratifying.

I watch every year as Shell employees take part in the Fund Raising Drive by Houston's Public Broadcasting Service. Most of the time, they wear their company's T-shirt as they take pledges over the phone from the public to support public television. It is a morale booster.

In his book entitled, *Aiming Higher – 25 stories of How Companies Prosper By Combining Sound Management and Social Vision,* David Bollier highlights how supporting social activities in communities pay great dividends to companies by improving employee attitudes in the workplace.

Engaging in community activities, either through company-sponsored programs or as an individual, is a morale booster and a great way to create positive attitudes in the workplace.

Chapter 11

MENTORS, MENTORSHIP AND ATTITUDE

I've learned that people will forget what you said, people will forget what you did, but people will never forget how you make them feel.

- Maya Angelou

Mentors have helped me be accountable. They've given me valuable advice, encouragement and direction. But most of all, they have made me feel proud of myself in whatever I have accomplished.

I have found that winning teams don't just happen. Whether they are on the playing field or on the job they are created and nurtured by some able hands that usually remain in the shadows, while the mentees enjoy the limelight. High-flying teams are built by skilled leaders who have mastered the art of mentoring to motivate, inspire and guide their people to success.

Mentoring is a tool used by organizations to nurture and grow their most valuable assets – people. This may be an informal practice or a formal program in which protégés observe, question, and explore, while mentors demonstrate, explain, and model. Importantly, they inspire the mentees to build a high level of confidence.

Mentoring is a joint venture, and for it to succeed, both parties have to understand their roles. It means sharing responsibility for learning. Regardless of the timing and anticipated accomplishments, it is a two-way street. Successful mentoring begins with setting a parameter for learning, which both the mentor and mentee must agree upon.

What makes mentoring good are the personal stories, examples, personal scenarios, and anecdotes, because they offer valuable, often unforgettable insight into what is to be learned. Mentors who can talk about themselves and their experiences establish a rapport that makes them "learning leaders."

Mentoring – if and when it works – taps into continuous learning that goes beyond ordinary events. Mentoring is an ongoing event combined with experience, observation, and studies.

One other important point to note is that mentoring focuses on the individual. Many a time, it does not follow a specific pattern because somewhere along the line, the mentor and mentee may discover some skills that the mentee did not know he/she had.

In order to bring about positive Attitude At Work, it is a good idea for people to be paired up with experienced employees who can serve as a guide to new employees. This method not only helps to bring people together to form good, sometime lifelong relationships both personally and professional, it also helps the organization save money while building a formidable, cohesive team.

Mentoring is particularly useful when properly organized for and by matured individuals, because unlike coaching, which is developed around a task, mentoring is developed around an individual. This gives it fluidity. Mentoring is not developed as an event or a program that is developed specifically for something, but a program that focuses on the individual. This practice is very flexible rather than something that is couched in a time frame. Therefore, mentoring is remarkably different from coaching.

If your organization does not promote a mentoring program, personally look for a mentor to help you in your quest for self development. It will cut your learning curve considerably.

Be A Mentor?

Being a mentor affords you the opportunity to have a great influence on the attitude of an employee, especially if that employee is new to the organization. On the other hand, if you are a mentee, you could cut your learning curve significantly by learning the ropes from an experienced employee who has been on the job for a considerable length of time. It helps you to go straight to what you want to learn rather than inventing the wheel, which may take a considerable amount of time.

Having a mentor improves your attitude. The mentor is your guide; he gives you the roadmap to navigate the company and helps you discover your own hidden skills.

Mentoring has been used since the beginning of man – from Moses to Joshua, Eli to Samuel, Elijah and Elisha, Paul and Timothy, Naomi and Ruth, and many others. It is a proven fact that if properly conducted, it can become a very useful tool to improve morale and engender a positive attitude in the workplace.

I want to make a brief comment on the reason why mentoring has not been widely embraced in corporate America. This is due to the fact that it brings people too close, much like big brother and big sister relationships. However, since these people are not blood kinship, proximity at times leads to all kinds of emotional problems.

Therefore, unless the people going into mentor/mentee relationships have the mature and emotional capabilities to handle the closeness and the sharing that is involved in mentoring, it should be avoided.

Properly organized, monitored and with appropriate emotional capabilities, mentoring can help to build great attitudes for employees, and create a very favorable atmosphere in the workplace that promotes positivity that spreads throughout the length and breadth of the company.

Chapter 12

DEALING WITH STRESS THROUGH POSITIVE ATTITUDE

Stress is like an iceberg. We can see one-eighth of it above, but what about what's below?

- Anonymous

Several studies have shown that stress can lead to all kinds of physical, emotional, social and psychological problems. The more stressed out people are, the more their attitude becomes negative and relationships at work suffer.

Stress can trigger negative attitudes. In a situation where more than one employee suffers from stress and displays bad attitude tendencies, the more caustic the atmosphere will become and the less job satisfaction employees will have.

In order to maintain a positive attitude in the workplace, efforts should be made to ensure that common causes of stress are eliminated or at least reduced. Once these are taken care of, employees can relax, relate well with one another, and do a good job.

According to Dr. Olufunke Odetunde, there are external stressors and internal stressors, some of which she identifies in her e-newsletters.

External stressors include

- Physical environment: noise, bright lights, heat, confined spaces.
- Social (interaction with people): rudeness, bossiness or aggression on the part of someone else.
- Organizational: rules, regulations, "red tape," deadlines.
- Major life events: death of a relative, job loss, promotion, new baby.
- Daily hassles: commuting, misplacing keys, mechanical breakdowns.

Internal stressors include

- Lifestyle choices: caffeine, not enough sleep, overloaded schedule.
- Negative self-talk: pessimistic thinking, self-criticism, over-analyzing.

- Mind traps: unrealistic expectations, taking things personally, all-or-nothing thinking, and exaggerating, rigid thinking.

Keeping the above causes in mind, let's take a look at some workplace causes of stress that affect employee attitudes.

- **Workload**: One of the greatest causes of stress in the workplace is the amount of workload an employee has to deal with. Not only will this cause an employee to be stressed out, if that employee senses that some other employees are not as busy as he is, and there is little or nothing he can do to correct the situation or the imbalance, it will eventually lead to stress, helplessness and a negative attitude. The employee may see himself as a victim. Unless this is controlled or investigated, such a negative attitude could spread to other employees who feel the same way as this particular employee. Before long the team will begin to have problems meeting deadlines. Managers must, therefore, ensure that work and responsibility are equally distributed among employees to avoid overworking a group while another group has very little to do. This will quickly bring about ill will, and the manager may be tagged as favoring a particular group over the other.

- **Phony Deadlines**: Phony deadlines are known to lead to stress among employees. This is a situation where the boss says an assignment is "urgent and important" making a particular employee work overtime, perhaps even spending part of his/her weekend to complete the assignment only to have it sitting and collecting dust on the manager's desk for another week or two, or in some extreme cases, totally discarded. A situation like this can frustrate an employee causing a great amount of stress. If such situations occur too frequently, it is possible that stress will occur and a negative attitude will result. Managers must, therefore, help to prioritize by setting genuine deadlines that are realistic. I used to talk about what I call "Drive-By Deadline." This is a deadline arbitrarily set by the boss who just walks up, drops a folder on the table saying, "Please let me have this back by the end of the day," without any explanation as to what is driving the "end of the day" deadline. When this happens, the employee is confused as he/she does not know which task is more important or urgent. Should he drop what he was doing before and take on this new task or should he continue with what he was doing and then get to this later? Any time a deadline is not driven by an external force (e.g. "I need this report at 4:00 p.m. so I can review it before I deliver it to the president in the morning" or "I need the software installed to enable me to format my manuscript to the book size I want") it should be considered an arbitrary deadline which may turn out to be a phony deadline.

- **Interruptions**: interruptions are the number one cause of stress in the workplace. These come in the form of phone calls, people dropping by or looking in while passing by. At times those interruptions are brought on by the employees themselves. Some employees create more interruptions for themselves through constant email checking and forwarding jokes, not making a day planner, not finishing one assignment before going on to another, pilling up assignments, etc. All of these things can cause stress. Each employee must devise a means of curbing interruptions. Employers too should ensure that interruptions are reduced to the barest minimum.

- **Change in the workplace**: Nothing causes more stress than when changes are being introduced (sometime at a very high frequency) without adequate explanation or communication as to why the changes are taking place and what is in them for the employees. When management fails to communicate early and long enough to make employees understand what the change means to them, employees begin to feel jittery. They are uncertain about their job, and this is reason for them to stress, which usually leads to poor attitude. To avoid this type of work-related stress, management must communicate early and adequately about change. Change must also be introduced piecemeal rather that in one fell-swoop. If changes are introduced a little at a time and the benefits are communicated to employees, stress will be reduced. Fear and uncertainty (which leads to negative attitudes) will be reduced or eliminated.
- **Favoritism**: Another source of stress for employees is when they see favoritism. When a manager favors one employee over another or a group of employees

over another, this definitely leads to stress and eventually to poor attitudes in the workplace. A good example is a manager who used to be one of the employees before being promoted. If the manager continues to go to lunch with his friends as before, some level of favoritism could be perceived or alleged by other employees, and this can bring problems to the team or lead to poor attitudes. Managers must be seen as fair. Treat team members with respect and without favoritism. Managers must refrain from socializing too much with certain groups over the others to avoid being accused of favoritism.

- **Lack of Direction**: People like to follow a leader who knows where he/she is going. A leader is one who has good policies that help the employees get their job done in a safe and helpful environment. It is not enough to have policies that cannot be enforced or are outdated. I once worked with a company that had an outdated sexual harassment policy that was very impractical. It lacked clarity and was so outdated that I felt the company was playing with fire. The policy did not take into consideration many of the new rules that have become part of the workplace in the last 10 or 15 years. It had not been updated in over five years. When I pointed this out, the manager said, “We are like a family here, and we don’t envisage anyone pulling such a stunt on us.” I quickly pointed out that people are usually friends and they are like a family until someone takes offence; then the whole friendship becomes fragmented and people who used to sing together will now shout at each other. To reduce fear and stress, therefore, every company must have well-written and easy-to-implement policies, and communicate them to the employees to make sure the policies are understood. This gives people direction as to what to do in case there is a problem. If you wait until there is a problem before you start looking for direction, you’ve waited too long. Policies are the roadmap. Therefore, give proper direction to the people. Have confidence and people will relax; pay attention to their duties rather than fretting and worrying about getting lost in the shuffle.

- **Communication**: “We don’t know what’s going on.” “Nobody is telling us anything.” “We just do what we are told; they don’t ask us for our opinion.”

These are just some of the complaints I get when I speak to employees. The employees feel helpless and powerless because no one is communicating or giving them any feedback on their job performance. In short, they are in the dark as to where they are or where they are going. Constant and immediate feedback helps to establish communication, which helps the employees know where they are and what is going on. When there is regular feedback, employees know what to expect in their annual performance reviews. I personally feel that some of the workplace violence can be prevented if employees know what is coming through regular communication. But when employees are shocked by a negative performance review which puts their career in a tailspin, they become nervous, stressed and lash out in violence. Communicate, communicate, communicate! Let people know where things stand at all times.

To reduce stress in the workplace, all efforts must be made to put people at ease, help them find fun to enable them to enjoy their work. Anything that aggravates employees, puts fear into their minds, or agitates them can cause stress and leads to violence.

Chapter 13

COMMUNICATING FOR RESULTS TO IMPROVE ATTITUDE

Misunderstandings don't exist; only failure to communicate exists.

-Proverbs

It has been discovered that your ability to communicate effectively, or lack thereof, can have a negative effect on your attitude and the attitudes of people around you in the workplace.

Effective communication is very important, and those who have acquired the skills enjoy considerable enjoyment in their workplace. Those who lack effective communication skills may get by, but are known to struggle with attitudinal problems.

Whatever profession you find yourself, you are constantly selling and buying. You may not be in sales, but selling is part of what you do, and to be successful, you have to have the ability to communicate effectively.

In the past, there were very few ways to communicate. In today's world, however, things have changed considerably. There are many different ways to communicate today, and many choices are available for you to choose. Depending on what medium you choose, your attitude may come into play.

Let's examine a few of the choices we have today without going into the history of communication.

In today's work environment, there is opportunity to communicate through telephone, video-phone, fax, email, instant messages, text messages or face-to-face.

Any of the above modes can be used to communicate, but for the purpose of our discussion, we will only concentrate on a few.

Telephone

Although the telephone has been around for almost a century, it is still the best means of communication next to face-to-face. Telephone communication has bridged the divide between people across the world. It is now possible to communicate with someone in a remote village or any place in the world.

Although you cannot see the person you are talking to on the phone, you can pick up nuances and vibes that will tell you a little bit about the person's attitude. It is possible to sense when a person at the other end of the line is giving you his/her 100% attention. In most cases, you can tell if the person is willing to help or is just trying to find a way to get you off the phone.

Just like it is possible to communicate enthusiasm through your voice, it is also possible to pick up disgust and impatience. The type of answers that come through the line can give your attitude away.

It is recommended that you project enthusiasm and friendliness on the phone through a little smile, which although your listener cannot see, he/she can pick up on the smile through your voice.

Face-To-Face Communication

The best form of communication is face-to-face. This is where you combine the use of all the senses and get the other person involved in the art of communication.

In face-to-face communication, your listener can see you, hear you, feel you and if possible, smell you.

When you communicate face-to-face, your attitude shows through. Everything is out in the open. You may try to hide a few things, but chances are, you are like an open book that can easily be read by your listener, because your employ all the senses we highlighted above and bring them to bear on the conversation.

Communicating Positive Attitude

Here are few things you can do to communicate positive attitude:

- Be Open: Being open is to make your listener feel welcome. This you can communicate through body language. An open hand, open face, open posture and relaxed body.
- Smile: "A smile is the brush that sweeps away the cobwebs of the heart." A little or big smile that is dancing on your face will make your eyes sparkle, and it is a great invitation to your listener to come in. It is telling your listener you are glad to see him or her and that you want to share what you have. A little smile (genuine, not a cheesy one) can disarm an otherwise hostile listener.
- Read your Listener: Reading your listener while communicating is very important because this is how you will find out if you are making sense or you are confusing the listener. You can tell whether your listener has a question or needs clarification on something. If you notice this, don't just keep on talking, instead stop and ask if your listener has a question.

- **Make Eye Contact**: Janet Jane once said, "Of all the things you wear, your facial expression is the most important." Making eye contact helps hold your listener's attention. You should also give your listener your full attention. Failure to make eye contact tells your listener that you are not very interested in him or that he is not invited in the conversation. Making eye contact, however, is a direct invitation.
- **Touch Your Listener Emotionally**: Whether you are speaking to one person or hundreds of people, to influence their attitude for the better, you must touch them emotionally. Most of what people do is ruled by emotions. Consequently, to improve people's attitudes in the workplace, you need to touch them emotionally. You can give people statistics, tell them about wonderful stuff, but if you fail to get them to commit emotionally, they will forget you in a split second. Remember, people will forget what you say, they will forget what you do, but they will never forget how you make them feel.

Observation of the above rules could help you to improve your attitude and people's attitudes tremendously.

Mistakes In Communication That Affect Attitude

To improve communication at work, which will eventually have an effect on your attitude, there are a few things to know and guide against.

1) **Assuming that your listener understands you:** This is by far one of the most egregious mistakes you can make at work, which may adversely affect your attitude. Any mistake in communication is a huge problem, but when that mistake is compounded by the fact that there is an assumption of understanding, which turns out to be wrong, then it becomes a dangerous thing. This type of communication problem generally occurs when the speaker or the person who originates the communication has the assumption that he is clear enough for someone to understand.

2) **Failure to Get Feedback:** The most egregious mistake you can make is to fail to get feedback from your listener to ensure understanding. This ties in with the first mistake because here again you

assume your listener understands. This can lead to serious problems. This problem generally occurs when two people fail to take the time to ask clarifying questions to check for understanding. Additionally, it could occur when the wrong question is asked, which will definitely elicit the wrong answer which appears to be right.

For example, if after you've explained a project to an assistant, and you ask him/her, "do you understand," chances are the assistant will say, "absolutely" or "yes." The question is, "Does he really understand?" Most of the time, the answer is "No." Don't be surprised to find the assistant looking for help from other people trying to find out if they understood what you said in the first place.

Or the assistant may sit for a while trying to figure out what you asked him. The point is that he is too shy, scared or doesn't want to look stupid, so he doesn't want to come back to ask you to repeat what you said.

The onus, however, is on you to explain what you want done in such a way that your listener will understand you. One way of checking for understanding is by asking the listener to tell you what you've just told him. That way, he will repeat the instruction back to you and both of you will be able to track down any misunderstanding and correct it before you leave the spot. Never ask, "Do you understand?" It is a failed policy. Instead ask, "What did I ask you to do?" "What do you understand I asked you to do?" "Or how do you understand what I asked you to do?

I was recently training a group of supervisors who work with men in construction. One of the supervisors shared a story where he had asked one of his men to cut off a valve. The man went in search of his chainsaw to cut the valve. What the supervisor meant was for the man to shut down the valve or close the valve. The supervisor happened to be around just when the employee was about to saw off the valve. It could have resulted in serious injury to the man and anyone within reach because the valve he was about to cut carried hot steam.

Yes, cut off and shut off could mean the same thing. The important thing is to make sure you are understood by asking clarifying questions.

Flash Me

A few years ago I was on the phone with a friend of mine who is a retired assistant district attorney. She was driving when I called, and because of the bad weather where she was, reception was poor. Our conversation was interrupted several times because of call-drops. Eventually I asked her where she was and she told me about the weather conditions. In response I said, "Why don't you *flash me* when you are at your destination and I can call you back."

As would be expected of an American woman, she went bananas and would have squeezed the life out of me if she could have gotten her hands on me, but I was too far away. She was angry and felt insulted. All the while I was wondering what I did wrong and why she was so angry with me.

It turned out that my statement for her to *flash me* was very offensive to her. It had a different meaning from what I intended.

"Flash me" is a common expression used in Nigeria and in many African countries. It is used by people who don't want to pay for a phone call. Read more about it here: http://blogs.mcclatchydc.com/nairobi/2007/09/flash-me.html.

It goes like this. Assuming you don't want to pay for a phone call in Nigeria or other African countries. You simply dial someone's number, let it ring once, twice and then you hang up, sit back and wait for the person to call you back. It is the person who makes the call that pays for the call. The person receiving pays nothing.

This is very common in countries outside the U.S. and that was what I had in mind when I asked my friend to "flash me." It took a few tries before we were able to sort things out where I could explain that I didn't say it to be rude or disrespectful.

The point is that many a time you say things and think that you are understood. Meanwhile, your listener is in the dark and unless you make an effort to clarify what you say, people will generally think they understand you, when in fact they do not. To make sure your message is received and understood as you intended, you must make an effort to get feedback to ensure proper understanding before you move on.

Here are some funny, but potentially dangerous experiences I have had with misunderstanding.

Learning To Swim In A New Stream

I had been in America for only a few weeks and I was attending my first job interview. The interview was going well until the lady asked me to stop saying "Yes Ma'am" to her.

I looked at her and said, "But you're older than me. Moreover, you're going to be my supervisor."

That was a big mistake on my part. Telling a woman she is older is a taboo in America. I didn't know that. She almost had a heart attack. I had been in the country for less than a month at this time.

We found a way to steer the interview back on course and nothing spectacular happened until I was about to leave her office.

We signed all the necessary papers; I had my copies. I knew when to report for duty. I thanked the lady (interviewer) and we shook hands. I was glad to leave.

I put my hand on the doorknob to open it and as if it was an afterthought, the lady said, "By the way, we require our associates to wear blue pants and white shirts."

This was innocent enough except that part of the statement had an entirely different meaning to me.

"What has blue pants got to do with my job?" I asked.

"It is company policy," she replied, looking askance.

"I don't understand," I said with a tinge in my voice.

"I just told you it is company policy," she repeated.

"Well, I don't have any blue pants because I don't wear them and I don't think I have the money to start shopping for blue pants now. As you can see, I'm trying to get my first job in America," I said getting a little angry.

She said nothing, so I continued.

"But, I still don't see why I have to wear blue pants. Are you saying that people run around the store in their pants?"

The poor lady looked at me more confused than ever. Obviously she was offended by my remarks just as I was horrified by the idea of having to discuss blue pants with a woman older than me, and my supervisor for that matter.

She looked at me again and asked, "What about those you are wearing?"

Knowing that I was wearing white "pants" and not blue "pants" I said, "You mean you can see through my trousers to what I'm wearing underneath? How did you know that, and by the way, you're wrong. I don't like this conversation, and I don't know what you are getting at."

At this point she was visibly angry just as I was, but something kept the two of us talking. She walked closer and pointed at my "trousers" and aksed, "What color are those?" I looked down and noticed that I was wearing a pair of Navy Blue "trousers."

Now that is a true story. My future supervisor was making a statement she thought I understood. As you see in the story, I had no clue what she was talking about. To me, pants meant underwear, not trousers.

That was before sexual harassment became popular. I could have lost the job even before I secured it simply because of misinterpretation or different understanding applied to a word by two innocent people.

The good thing about that episode was that we were able to solve the miscommunication problem on the spot. Otherwise, it would have poisoned the atmosphere for the two of us in the workplace and it would have definitely affected our attitudes toward each other.

Your ability to communicate or lack thereof can have a profound effect on your attitude in the workplace.

To avoid this type of miscommunication, follow these suggestions:

- Speak clearly
- Avoid jargon when you speak
- If possible, use more than one word to describe what you are saying
- Listen attentively
- Avoid words with ambiguous meanings
- Ask clarifying questions to ensure understanding
- Make your listener restate your statement to you in his or her own words to ensure understanding
- Don't assume understanding just because someone says he understands
- Get feedback
- Follow up and follow through.

Always remember that communication is tough, therefore, it must be taken very seriously and handled with care. A little misunderstanding could lead to thousands of dollars in damage or lead to someone's death.

Acquiring good communication skills is a must for anyone who wants to improve his attitude at work because poor communication skills can cause an otherwise good worker to become cynical and display a negative attitude.

Therefore, before you make a statement and think you are understood, find out the background of your listeners and get feedback to ensure understanding.

The most important thing to remember is that "Misunderstandings don't exist; only failure to communication exists." Meaning that the responsibility to be understood is placed on you, the speaker. It is your duty to make sure you are understood and that your message is received and understood as intended.

Therefore, if you want to improve your attitude and get the best out of your work day, you must learn to acquire good communication skills, which will in turn help you improve your attitude and save you the headaches that go with poor attitude in the workplace.

Show Benefits

One of the best ways to give people a reason to listen to you is to show benefits. Take the people to the most popular radio station in the world WIIFM (What's In It For Me?). When people begin to ask that question, let them find an answer in your words. If your listeners can see what they stand to gain by your communication, they will listen.

Communicate Value and Importance

If you want to influence people's attitudes and your own attitude for the best in the workplace, communicate value and importance.

This you do by letting people feel that you value them, their opinions and their contributions and that they are important to the organization. By doing this, you will make them feel important. People will forget what you say. They will likely forget what you do, but they will never forget how you make them feel when they are with you or listen to you. This in itself is a morale booster and it brings about positive attitude.

Chapter 14

GETTING ORGANIZED

I couldn't have done what I have done without the habits of punctuality, order and diligence.

- Charles Dickens

Being organized can have a significant effect on your attitude. Studies have shown that the average person spends several hours each year searching for misplaced or lost objects or looking for information. This is a problem that getting a little organized can help you resolve.

Getting organized is not merely about keeping things in the right place. It also involves doing first things first and taking on tasks in such a way that you are not overwhelmed by the task which usually leads to procrastination. People procrastinate when they don't know what to do or how to do what they need to do, but most of all, when they are overwhelmed.

Dealing With Procrastination

This is one of the thieves of your time as described by William Shakespeare. It has a way of eating into your time under the excuse that you have no time.

For example, as you read this chapter, right now, if I were to walk into your garage, what would I find? Chances are I would find boxes and boxes of stuff. Things you've been keeping since you left high school 35 years ago. Things you've been promising yourself you would use someday, but you've never had any need for and yet are very reluctant to throw away.

I would likely find more stuff that has taken over your two-car garage to the extent that you can no longer park your cars in your garage, instead your cars stay in your driveway. If they could talk, they would be yelling at you to take them out of the heat or cold depending on where you live.

A little conversation of why you've been keeping all the stuff for so long would probably produce a reason or an excuse why those boxes have been there for so long. Something like, "I've been promising myself that I would get them sorted out some day, but there are so many boxes and I don't even know where to start."

Now it has become a hindrance for you. You can't even walk into your garage anymore because there is stuff all over the place. You can't find anything in the garage. It is irritating you to see your garage like that, and it is getting on your nerves. How to handle it?

There is an old African story that can help you get over the hump.

A boy came to play with his friends one morning. He was so excited when he arrived that his friends wondered what had come over him. They were forced to ask:

"Why are you so excited today?"

"I'm excited because I'm going to eat an elephant."

His friends laughed at him. They reminded him that an elephant is a huge animal. "But you are very small," they chided him. "How in the world are you going to eat an elephant anyway, Mr. Big Mouth?"

The boy simply answered, "One bite at a time."

If you would follow this advice, take one box down every week and sort out the contents, and in no time, you will have cleared your garage of all the junk. This is also akin to what they call, "divide and conquer."

Go ahead, try it, and you will see an improvement in your attitude both at home and at work as you begin to get rid of the junk – a little at a time.

Critical Tips for staying organized

- Plan your work and work your plan
- Do first things first by prioritizing
- Handle what brings you the most value first
- Delegate as much as you can
- Avoid interruption both internal and external
- Do your best work when you are at your best
- Constantly revise your "to do" list
- Set realistic goals and deadlines
- Plan your tomorrow today
- Set time aside for play and relaxation
- Celebrate every accomplishment
- Work your priorities first
- Use the divide and conquer rule (eating an elephant)

- Trash it if you won't need it
- Deal with paper only once (File it, send it out or toss it)
- Schedule it and it will get done

Remember that for every minute you spend organizing, you earn an hour. It is imperative to organize and stay organize if expect to have some sanity in your activities.

CONCLUSION

Good attitudes do not guarantee success, but negative attitudes guarantee ruin.

To enjoy work and play, it is imperative that you project a good attitude that will allow you to love and enjoy your work and build good interpersonal relationships with people around you.

Always remember that hard work can only give you 98% while attitude gives you 100%. At the end of the day, it is your attitude that will make or break you. It is your attitude that makes all the difference.

If you have a good attitude, you will enjoy a good working environment, cooperation from co-workers and most of all, a boss who sees you as a partner rather than another problem to deal with.

Hey, attitude is contagious! Make sure you are catching the right one and then spread it like a ripple in the water.

As my grandfather used to say, “You can’t change the direction of the wind and the water current, but you can adjust your sails." Adjusting your attitude will get you to your destination faster and safer.

Good Luck!

About the Author

Ola Joseph, M.A., DTM heads his own consulting firm in Houston Texas. He is a nationally known keynote speaker, executive speech coach and trainer. Ola has helped many business leaders and organizations enhance their success through hands-on coaching and mentoring. A dynamic and unique speaker, Ola has spoken before many conference and corporate audiences. He is a writer with nine best selling books and over 50 published magazine and newspaper articles. He is a member of the National Association of Judiciary interpreters and Translators in three languages, Houston Organization Development Network, Houston Association of Black Journalists and Toastmasters International. He is also a certified Oral Proficiency Tester with the American Council on the Teaching of Foreign Languages.

For more Info on how to get Ola to speak at your conference or conduct training workshop, mentoring and coaching, please call:

Ola Joseph

Tel: 713 283 5141

Tel: 713 471 6812

ola@olayinka.com

ola.talks@juno.com

www.olayinka.com

RIVERBANK & ASSOCIATES

Ola's company, Riverbank & Associates helps individuals and organizations deal with change, communicate more effectively and inspire them to be way above normal. Every presentation includes a unique blend of humor, stories and examples to inspire, motivate and educate the audience. Call today!

Keynote Speeches

- Attitude At Work
- Wind of Change In The Air
- Take The Leap of Faith
- Soaring On The Wings of Courage

Workshops

- Attitude At Work: How to give yourself permission to love your job
- Personal & Professional Development Workshops
- The Golden Nuggets of Platform Power In Public Speaking
- Turn Your Accent Into An Asset – Communicate effectively even if English is not your first language
- Change Management Workshops
- Mentoring and Mentorship Training

Services for Professional and Business Executives

- Personal and Executive Speech Coaching
- Interpreting and translation services
- Individualized Mentoring/Coaching
- Book writing services

www.olayinka.com
E-mail: ola@olayinka.com
Tel: 713 283 5141
P. O. Box 721791
Houston, TX 77272-1791

ORDER FORM (Copy this form, fill it out & mail)

For additional copies of this book, please go to www.olayinka.com or send an e-mail/or your request to ola.talks@juno.com or ola@olayinka.com, call 713 283 5141.

Indigo Riverbank Books, TX
P. O. Box 721791, Houston, TX 77272-1791
Tel: (713) 283-5141

# Copies	**Price**	**U.S. Shipping/Handling**
1 Paperback	$19.95 each	$5.50 first book/CD
10 + copies (20% discount)		50 + copies (40% discount)

International Orders Shipping/handling:

Surface: $35.00 for the first book/CD
$18.00 each additional book

No COD Orders

… of books x cost per book = total: $……………………
Shipping/handling $……………......
Texas residents add 8.25% sales tax $……………........

Grand Total $===========

Payment: Check#:…………….. Amount $…..………….
Credit Card: VISA ___ MC ___ AMEX ____ DISC _____

Card#. ……………………………. Exp. Date …………......
Name on Card: ……………………...Sign...…...………..
Billing /Shipping Address:
Name: ____

Shipping Address:_____________________________________

City: ______State: ____Zip:___ Phone ( )_________________

OTHER BOOKS BY OLAYINKA JOSEPH

GET A FREE GIFT

If you bought this book at a bookstore, Amazon.com or on the internet, please fill out this form and mail it in for our monthly drawings for free consultations (a $175 Value).

Name: ……………………………………………………………….....

Address: ……………………………………………………..............

………………………………………………………………………

Tel: …………………………………………………………..............

Email Address: ………………………………………….............

NEED PERSONAL DEVELOPMENT? Visit:

www.olayinka.com

Please send to:

Ola Joseph
Riverbank & Associates
Indigo Riverbank Books, TX
P. O. Box 721791
Houston, TX 77272-1791

Further reading

- Secrets of Executive Success – Rodale Center for Executive Development
- Wind of Change In The Air – Olayinka Joseph
- Attitude 101 – John c. Maxwell
- Turn Your Accent Into An Asset – Olayinka Joseph
- Think Like a Manager – Roger Fritz
- Unleashing the Power of Everyday Leadership – Hal Pitt
- I Dare You – Olayinka Joseph
- The Forbes Book of Business Quotations
- Leader Reach – Bonnie V. Banks